# 30 DAYS *challenge tracker*

**CHALLENGE**

📅 STARTING DATE:

📅 END DATE:

**REWARD**

**I CAN MAKE IT!**

| | | | | | | |
|---|---|---|---|---|---|---|
| 1 | 2 | 3 | 4 | 5 | 6 | 7 |
| 8 | 9 | 10 | 11 | 12 | 13 | 14 |
| 15 | 16 | 17 | 18 | 19 | 20 | 21 |
| 22 | 23 | 24 | 25 | 26 | 27 | 28 |

29  30  **I DID IT!**

**NOTE**

**PLAN OF ACTION**

**HOW WILL IT BENEFIT ME?**

1.
2.
3.
4.
5.
6.
7.
8.
10.
11.
12.

# 30 DAYS *challenge tracker*

**CHALLENGE**

📅 STARTING DATE:

📅 END DATE:

**REWARD**

I CAN MAKE IT!

| 1 | 2 | 3 | 4 | 5 | 6 | 7 |

| 8 | 9 | 10 | 11 | 12 | 13 | 14 |

| 15 | 16 | 17 | 18 | 19 | 20 | 21 |

| 22 | 23 | 24 | 25 | 26 | 27 | 28 |

29 | 30 | I DID IT!

**NOTE**

**PLAN OF ACTION**

**HOW WILL IT BENEFIT ME?**

1.
2.
3.
4.
5.
6.
7.
8.
10.
11.
12.

# 30 DAYS *challenge tracker*

**CHALLENGE**

📅 STARTING DATE:

📅 END DATE:

**REWARD**

**I CAN MAKE IT!**

( 1 ) ( 2 ) ( 3 ) ( 4 ) ( 5 ) ( 6 ) ( 7 )

( 8 ) ( 9 ) ( 10 ) ( 11 ) ( 12 ) ( 13 ) ( 14 )

( 15 ) ( 16 ) ( 17 ) ( 18 ) ( 19 ) ( 20 ) ( 21 )

( 22 ) ( 23 ) ( 24 ) ( 25 ) ( 26 ) ( 27 ) ( 28 )

( 29 ) ( 30 ) **I DID IT!**

**NOTE**

**PLAN OF ACTION**

**HOW WILL IT BENEFIT ME?**

1.
2.
3.
4.
5.
6.
7.
8.
10.
11.
12.

# 30 DAYS *challenge tracker*

**CHALLENGE**

STARTING DATE:

END DATE:

**REWARD**

**I CAN MAKE IT!**

( 1 ) ( 2 ) ( 3 ) ( 4 ) ( 5 ) ( 6 ) ( 7 )

( 8 ) ( 9 ) ( 10 ) ( 11 ) ( 12 ) ( 13 ) ( 14 )

( 15 ) ( 16 ) ( 17 ) ( 18 ) ( 19 ) ( 20 ) ( 21 )

( 22 ) ( 23 ) ( 24 ) ( 25 ) ( 26 ) ( 27 ) ( 28 )

( 29 ) ( 30 ) **I DID IT!**

**NOTE**

**PLAN OF ACTION**

**HOW WILL IT BENEFIT ME?**

1.
2.
3.
4.
5.
6.
7.
8.
10.
11.
12.

# 30 DAYS *challenge tracker*

**CHALLENGE**

📅 STARTING DATE:

📅 END DATE:

**REWARD**

**I CAN MAKE IT!**

( 1 ) — ( 2 ) — ( 3 ) — ( 4 ) — ( 5 ) — ( 6 ) — ( 7 )

( 8 ) — ( 9 ) — ( 10 ) — ( 11 ) — ( 12 ) — ( 13 ) — ( 14 )

( 15 ) — ( 16 ) — ( 17 ) — ( 18 ) — ( 19 ) — ( 20 ) — ( 21 )

( 22 ) — ( 23 ) — ( 24 ) — ( 25 ) — ( 26 ) — ( 27 ) — ( 28 )

( 29 ) — ( 30 ) **I DID IT!**

**NOTE**

**PLAN OF ACTION**

**HOW WILL IT BENEFIT ME?**

1.
2.
3.
4.
5.
6.
7.
8.
10.
11.
12.

# 30 DAYS *challenge tracker*

**CHALLENGE**

📅 STARTING DATE:

📅 END DATE:

**REWARD**

**I CAN MAKE IT!**

( 1 ) ( 2 ) ( 3 ) ( 4 ) ( 5 ) ( 6 ) ( 7 )

( 8 ) ( 9 ) ( 10 ) ( 11 ) ( 12 ) ( 13 ) ( 14 )

( 15 ) ( 16 ) ( 17 ) ( 18 ) ( 19 ) ( 20 ) ( 21 )

( 22 ) ( 23 ) ( 24 ) ( 25 ) ( 26 ) ( 27 ) ( 28 )

( 29 ) ( 30 ) **I DID IT!**

**NOTE**

**PLAN OF ACTION**

☐
☐
☐
☐
☐
☐
☐

**HOW WILL IT BENEFIT ME?**

1.
2.
3.
4.
5.
6.
7.
8.
10.
11.
12.

# 30 DAYS *challenge tracker*

**CHALLENGE**

STARTING DATE:

END DATE:

**REWARD**

**I CAN MAKE IT!**

( 1 ) ( 2 ) ( 3 ) ( 4 ) ( 5 ) ( 6 ) ( 7 )

( 8 ) ( 9 ) ( 10 ) ( 11 ) ( 12 ) ( 13 ) ( 14 )

( 15 ) ( 16 ) ( 17 ) ( 18 ) ( 19 ) ( 20 ) ( 21 )

( 22 ) ( 23 ) ( 24 ) ( 25 ) ( 26 ) ( 27 ) ( 28 )

( 29 ) ( 30 ) **I DID IT!**

**NOTE**

**PLAN OF ACTION**

**HOW WILL IT BENEFIT ME?**

1.
2.
3.
4.
5.
6.
7.
8.
10.
11.
12.

# 30 DAYS *challenge tracker*

**CHALLENGE**

**REWARD**

📅 STARTING DATE:

📅 END DATE:

I CAN MAKE IT!

( 1 ) ( 2 ) ( 3 ) ( 4 ) ( 5 ) ( 6 ) ( 7 )

( 8 ) ( 9 ) ( 10 ) ( 11 ) ( 12 ) ( 13 ) ( 14 )

( 15 ) ( 16 ) ( 17 ) ( 18 ) ( 19 ) ( 20 ) ( 21 )

( 22 ) ( 23 ) ( 24 ) ( 25 ) ( 26 ) ( 27 ) ( 28 )

( 29 ) ( 30 ) I DID IT!

**NOTE**

**PLAN OF ACTION**

**HOW WILL IT BENEFIT ME?**

1.
2.
3.
4.
5.
6.
7.
8.
10.
11.
12.

# 30 DAYS *challenge tracker*

**CHALLENGE**

📅 STARTING DATE:

📅 END DATE:

**REWARD**

**I CAN MAKE IT!**

( 1 ) ( 2 ) ( 3 ) ( 4 ) ( 5 ) ( 6 ) ( 7 )

( 8 ) ( 9 ) ( 10 ) ( 11 ) ( 12 ) ( 13 ) ( 14 )

( 15 ) ( 16 ) ( 17 ) ( 18 ) ( 19 ) ( 20 ) ( 21 )

( 22 ) ( 23 ) ( 24 ) ( 25 ) ( 26 ) ( 27 ) ( 28 )

( 29 ) ( 30 ) **I DID IT!**

**NOTE**

**PLAN OF ACTION**

**HOW WILL IT BENEFIT ME?**

1.
2.
3.
4.
5.
6.
7.
8.
10.
11.
12.

# 30 DAYS *challenge tracker*

**CHALLENGE**

📅 STARTING DATE:

📅 END DATE:

**REWARD**

I CAN MAKE IT!

( 1 ) — ( 2 ) — ( 3 ) — ( 4 ) — ( 5 ) — ( 6 ) — ( 7 )

( 8 ) — ( 9 ) — ( 10 ) — ( 11 ) — ( 12 ) — ( 13 ) — ( 14 )

( 15 ) — ( 16 ) — ( 17 ) — ( 18 ) — ( 19 ) — ( 20 ) — ( 21 )

( 22 ) — ( 23 ) — ( 24 ) — ( 25 ) — ( 26 ) — ( 27 ) — ( 28 )

( 29 ) — ( 30 ) I DID IT!

**NOTE**

**PLAN OF ACTION**

**HOW WILL IT BENEFIT ME?**

1.
2.
3.
4.
5.
6.
7.
8.
10.
11.
12.

# 30 DAYS *challenge tracker*

**CHALLENGE**

📅 STARTING DATE:

📅 END DATE:

**REWARD**

**I CAN MAKE IT!**

( 1 ) ( 2 ) ( 3 ) ( 4 ) ( 5 ) ( 6 ) ( 7 )

( 8 ) ( 9 ) ( 10 ) ( 11 ) ( 12 ) ( 13 ) ( 14 )

( 15 ) ( 16 ) ( 17 ) ( 18 ) ( 19 ) ( 20 ) ( 21 )

( 22 ) ( 23 ) ( 24 ) ( 25 ) ( 26 ) ( 27 ) ( 28 )

( 29 ) ( 30 ) **I DID IT!**

**NOTE**

**PLAN OF ACTION**

**HOW WILL IT BENEFIT ME?**

1.
2.
3.
4.
5.
6.
7.
8.
10.
11.
12.

# 30 DAYS *challenge tracker*

**CHALLENGE**

STARTING DATE:

END DATE:

**REWARD**

I CAN MAKE IT!

( 1 ) ( 2 ) ( 3 ) ( 4 ) ( 5 ) ( 6 ) ( 7 )

( 8 ) ( 9 ) ( 10 ) ( 11 ) ( 12 ) ( 13 ) ( 14 )

( 15 ) ( 16 ) ( 17 ) ( 18 ) ( 19 ) ( 20 ) ( 21 )

( 22 ) ( 23 ) ( 24 ) ( 25 ) ( 26 ) ( 27 ) ( 28 )

( 29 ) ( 30 ) I DID IT!

**NOTE**

**PLAN OF ACTION**

**HOW WILL IT BENEFIT ME?**

1.
2.
3.
4.
5.
6.
7.
8.
10.
11.
12.

# 30 DAYS *challenge tracker*

**CHALLENGE**

STARTING DATE:

END DATE:

**REWARD**

**I CAN MAKE IT!**

1 — 2 — 3 — 4 — 5 — 6 — 7

8 — 9 — 10 — 11 — 12 — 13 — 14

15 — 16 — 17 — 18 — 19 — 20 — 21

22 — 23 — 24 — 25 — 26 — 27 — 28

29 — 30 — **I DID IT!**

**NOTE**

**PLAN OF ACTION**

**HOW WILL IT BENEFIT ME?**

1.
2.
3.
4.
5.
6.
7.
8.
10.
11.
12.

# 30 DAYS *challenge tracker*

**CHALLENGE**

STARTING DATE:

END DATE:

**REWARD**

**I CAN MAKE IT!**

| 1 | 2 | 3 | 4 | 5 | 6 | 7 |
| 8 | 9 | 10 | 11 | 12 | 13 | 14 |
| 15 | 16 | 17 | 18 | 19 | 20 | 21 |
| 22 | 23 | 24 | 25 | 26 | 27 | 28 |

29 | 30 | **I DID IT!**

**NOTE**

## PLAN OF ACTION

## HOW WILL IT BENEFIT ME?

1.
2.
3.
4.
5.
6.
7.
8.
10.
11.
12.

# 30 DAYS *challenge tracker*

**CHALLENGE**

📅 STARTING DATE:

📅 END DATE:

**REWARD**

I CAN MAKE IT!

( 1 ) ( 2 ) ( 3 ) ( 4 ) ( 5 ) ( 6 ) ( 7 )

( 8 ) ( 9 ) ( 10 ) ( 11 ) ( 12 ) ( 13 ) ( 14 )

( 15 ) ( 16 ) ( 17 ) ( 18 ) ( 19 ) ( 20 ) ( 21 )

( 22 ) ( 23 ) ( 24 ) ( 25 ) ( 26 ) ( 27 ) ( 28 )

( 29 ) ( 30 ) I DID IT!

**NOTE**

**PLAN OF ACTION**

**HOW WILL IT BENEFIT ME?**

1.
2.
3.
4.
5.
6.
7.
8.
10.
11.
12.

# 30 DAYS *challenge tracker*

**CHALLENGE**

📅 STARTING DATE:

📅 END DATE:

**REWARD**

**I CAN MAKE IT!**

1 — 2 — 3 — 4 — 5 — 6 — 7

8 — 9 — 10 — 11 — 12 — 13 — 14

15 — 16 — 17 — 18 — 19 — 20 — 21

22 — 23 — 24 — 25 — 26 — 27 — 28

29 — 30   **I DID IT!**

**NOTE**

**PLAN OF ACTION**

**HOW WILL IT BENEFIT ME?**

1.
2.
3.
4.
5.
6.
7.
8.
10.
11.
12.

# 30 DAYS *challenge tracker*

**CHALLENGE**

📅 STARTING DATE:

📅 END DATE:

**REWARD**

**I CAN MAKE IT!**

( 1 ) ( 2 ) ( 3 ) ( 4 ) ( 5 ) ( 6 ) ( 7 )

( 8 ) ( 9 ) ( 10 ) ( 11 ) ( 12 ) ( 13 ) ( 14 )

( 15 ) ( 16 ) ( 17 ) ( 18 ) ( 19 ) ( 20 ) ( 21 )

( 22 ) ( 23 ) ( 24 ) ( 25 ) ( 26 ) ( 27 ) ( 28 )

( 29 ) ( 30 ) **I DID IT!**

**NOTE**

**PLAN OF ACTION**

**HOW WILL IT BENEFIT ME?**

1.
2.
3.
4.
5.
6.
7.
8.
10.
11.
12.

# 30 DAYS *challenge tracker*

## CHALLENGE

STARTING DATE:

END DATE:

## REWARD

I CAN MAKE IT!

( 1 ) ( 2 ) ( 3 ) ( 4 ) ( 5 ) ( 6 ) ( 7 )

( 8 ) ( 9 ) ( 10 ) ( 11 ) ( 12 ) ( 13 ) ( 14 )

( 15 ) ( 16 ) ( 17 ) ( 18 ) ( 19 ) ( 20 ) ( 21 )

( 22 ) ( 23 ) ( 24 ) ( 25 ) ( 26 ) ( 27 ) ( 28 )

( 29 ) ( 30 ) I DID IT!

## NOTE

## PLAN OF ACTION

## HOW WILL IT BENEFIT ME?

1.
2.
3.
4.
5.
6.
7.
8.
10.
11.
12.

# 30 DAYS *challenge tracker*

**CHALLENGE**

📅 STARTING DATE:

📅 END DATE:

**REWARD**

**I CAN MAKE IT!**

( 1 ) ( 2 ) ( 3 ) ( 4 ) ( 5 ) ( 6 ) ( 7 )

( 8 ) ( 9 ) ( 10 ) ( 11 ) ( 12 ) ( 13 ) ( 14 )

( 15 ) ( 16 ) ( 17 ) ( 18 ) ( 19 ) ( 20 ) ( 21 )

( 22 ) ( 23 ) ( 24 ) ( 25 ) ( 26 ) ( 27 ) ( 28 )

( 29 ) ( 30 ) **I DID IT!**

**NOTE**

**PLAN OF ACTION**

**HOW WILL IT BENEFIT ME?**

1.
2.
3.
4.
5.
6.
7.
8.
10.
11.
12.

# 30 DAYS *challenge tracker*

**CHALLENGE**

**STARTING DATE:**

**END DATE:**

**REWARD**

**I CAN MAKE IT!**

( 1 ) ( 2 ) ( 3 ) ( 4 ) ( 5 ) ( 6 ) ( 7 )

( 8 ) ( 9 ) ( 10 ) ( 11 ) ( 12 ) ( 13 ) ( 14 )

( 15 ) ( 16 ) ( 17 ) ( 18 ) ( 19 ) ( 20 ) ( 21 )

( 22 ) ( 23 ) ( 24 ) ( 25 ) ( 26 ) ( 27 ) ( 28 )

( 29 ) ( 30 ) **I DID IT!**

**NOTE**

## PLAN OF ACTION

## HOW WILL IT BENEFIT ME?

1.
2.
3.
4.
5.
6.
7.
8.
10.
11.
12.

# 30 DAYS *challenge tracker*

**CHALLENGE**

📅 STARTING DATE:

📅 END DATE:

**REWARD**

I CAN MAKE IT!

( 1 ) ( 2 ) ( 3 ) ( 4 ) ( 5 ) ( 6 ) ( 7 )

( 8 ) ( 9 ) ( 10 ) ( 11 ) ( 12 ) ( 13 ) ( 14 )

( 15 ) ( 16 ) ( 17 ) ( 18 ) ( 19 ) ( 20 ) ( 21 )

( 22 ) ( 23 ) ( 24 ) ( 25 ) ( 26 ) ( 27 ) ( 28 )

( 29 ) ( 30 ) I DID IT!

**NOTE**

**PLAN OF ACTION**

**HOW WILL IT BENEFIT ME?**

1.
2.
3.
4.
5.
6.
7.
8.
10.
11.
12.

# 30 DAYS *challenge tracker*

**CHALLENGE**

**STARTING DATE:**

**END DATE:**

**REWARD**

I CAN MAKE IT!

( 1 ) — ( 2 ) — ( 3 ) — ( 4 ) — ( 5 ) — ( 6 ) — ( 7 )

( 8 ) — ( 9 ) — ( 10 ) — ( 11 ) — ( 12 ) — ( 13 ) — ( 14 )

( 15 ) — ( 16 ) — ( 17 ) — ( 18 ) — ( 19 ) — ( 20 ) — ( 21 )

( 22 ) — ( 23 ) — ( 24 ) — ( 25 ) — ( 26 ) — ( 27 ) — ( 28 )

( 29 ) — ( 30 )  I DID IT!

**NOTE**

**PLAN OF ACTION**

**HOW WILL IT BENEFIT ME?**

1.
2.
3.
4.
5.
6.
7.
8.
10.
11.
12.

# 30 DAYS *challenge tracker*

**CHALLENGE**

STARTING DATE:

END DATE:

**REWARD**

I CAN MAKE IT!

1 — 2 — 3 — 4 — 5 — 6 — 7

8 — 9 — 10 — 11 — 12 — 13 — 14

15 — 16 — 17 — 18 — 19 — 20 — 21

22 — 23 — 24 — 25 — 26 — 27 — 28

29 — 30   I DID IT!

**NOTE**

**PLAN OF ACTION**

**HOW WILL IT BENEFIT ME?**

1.
2.
3.
4.
5.
6.
7.
8.
10.
11.
12.

# 30 DAYS *challenge tracker*

**CHALLENGE**

STARTING DATE:

END DATE:

**REWARD**

**I CAN MAKE IT!**

1 — 2 — 3 — 4 — 5 — 6 — 7

8 — 9 — 10 — 11 — 12 — 13 — 14

15 — 16 — 17 — 18 — 19 — 20 — 21

22 — 23 — 24 — 25 — 26 — 27 — 28

29 — 30   **I DID IT!**

**NOTE**

## PLAN OF ACTION

## HOW WILL IT BENEFIT ME?

1.
2.
3.
4.
5.
6.
7.
8.
10.
11.
12.

# 30 DAYS *challenge tracker*

**CHALLENGE**

STARTING DATE:

END DATE:

**REWARD**

**I CAN MAKE IT!**

① 1 — 2 — 3 — 4 — 5 — 6 — 7

8 — 9 — 10 — 11 — 12 — 13 — 14

15 — 16 — 17 — 18 — 19 — 20 — 21

22 — 23 — 24 — 25 — 26 — 27 — 28

29 — 30    **I DID IT!**

**NOTE**

**PLAN OF ACTION**

**HOW WILL IT BENEFIT ME?**

1.
2.
3.
4.
5.
6.
7.
8.
10.
11.
12.

# 30 DAYS *challenge tracker*

**CHALLENGE**

📅 STARTING DATE:

📅 END DATE:

**REWARD**

I CAN MAKE IT!
① ② ③ ④ ⑤ ⑥ ⑦
⑧ ⑨ ⑩ ⑪ ⑫ ⑬ ⑭
⑮ ⑯ ⑰ ⑱ ⑲ ⑳ ㉑
㉒ ㉓ ㉔ ㉕ ㉖ ㉗ ㉘
㉙ ㉚ I DID IT!

**NOTE**

**PLAN OF ACTION**

**HOW WILL IT BENEFIT ME?**

1.
2.
3.
4.
5.
6.
7.
8.
10.
11.
12.

# 30 DAYS *challenge tracker*

**CHALLENGE**

**STARTING DATE:**

**END DATE:**

**REWARD**

I CAN MAKE IT!

( 1 )—( 2 )—( 3 )—( 4 )—( 5 )—( 6 )—( 7 )

( 8 )—( 9 )—( 10 )—( 11 )—( 12 )—( 13 )—( 14 )

( 15 )—( 16 )—( 17 )—( 18 )—( 19 )—( 20 )—( 21 )

( 22 )—( 23 )—( 24 )—( 25 )—( 26 )—( 27 )—( 28 )

( 29 )—( 30 )  I DID IT!

**NOTE**

## PLAN OF ACTION

## HOW WILL IT BENEFIT ME?

1.
2.
3.
4.
5.
6.
7.
8.
10.
11.
12.

# 30 DAYS *challenge tracker*

**CHALLENGE**

📅 STARTING DATE:

📅 END DATE:

**REWARD**

I CAN MAKE IT!

( 1 ) ( 2 ) ( 3 ) ( 4 ) ( 5 ) ( 6 ) ( 7 )

( 8 ) ( 9 ) ( 10 ) ( 11 ) ( 12 ) ( 13 ) ( 14 )

( 15 ) ( 16 ) ( 17 ) ( 18 ) ( 19 ) ( 20 ) ( 21 )

( 22 ) ( 23 ) ( 24 ) ( 25 ) ( 26 ) ( 27 ) ( 28 )

( 29 ) ( 30 ) I DID IT!

**NOTE**

**PLAN OF ACTION**

**HOW WILL IT BENEFIT ME?**

1.
2.
3.
4.
5.
6.
7.
8.
10.
11.
12.

# 30 DAYS *challenge tracker*

**CHALLENGE**

📅 STARTING DATE:

📅 END DATE:

**REWARD**

**I CAN MAKE IT!**

( 1 ) ( 2 ) ( 3 ) ( 4 ) ( 5 ) ( 6 ) ( 7 )

( 8 ) ( 9 ) ( 10 ) ( 11 ) ( 12 ) ( 13 ) ( 14 )

( 15 ) ( 16 ) ( 17 ) ( 18 ) ( 19 ) ( 20 ) ( 21 )

( 22 ) ( 23 ) ( 24 ) ( 25 ) ( 26 ) ( 27 ) ( 28 )

( 29 ) ( 30 ) **I DID IT!**

**NOTE**

**PLAN OF ACTION**

**HOW WILL IT BENEFIT ME?**

1.
2.
3.
4.
5.
6.
7.
8.
10.
11.
12.

# 30 DAYS *challenge tracker*

**CHALLENGE**

**REWARD**

📅 STARTING DATE:

📅 END DATE:

I CAN MAKE IT! ① ② ③ ④ ⑤ ⑥ ⑦

⑧ ⑨ ⑩ ⑪ ⑫ ⑬ ⑭

⑮ ⑯ ⑰ ⑱ ⑲ ⑳ 21

22 23 24 25 26 27 28

29 30 I DID IT!

**NOTE**

**PLAN OF ACTION**

☐
☐
☐
☐
☐
☐
☐
☐

**HOW WILL IT BENEFIT ME?**

1.
2.
3.
4.
5.
6.
7.
8.
10.
11.
12.

# 30 DAYS *challenge tracker*

**CHALLENGE**

📅 STARTING DATE:

📅 END DATE:

**REWARD**

I CAN MAKE IT!

( 1 )—( 2 )—( 3 )—( 4 )—( 5 )—( 6 )—( 7 )

( 8 )—( 9 )—( 10 )—( 11 )—( 12 )—( 13 )—( 14 )

( 15 )—( 16 )—( 17 )—( 18 )—( 19 )—( 20 )—( 21 )

( 22 )—( 23 )—( 24 )—( 25 )—( 26 )—( 27 )—( 28 )

( 29 )—( 30 )  I DID IT!

**NOTE**

**PLAN OF ACTION**

**HOW WILL IT BENEFIT ME?**

1.
2.
3.
4.
5.
6.
7.
8.
10.
11.
12.

# 30 DAYS *challenge tracker*

**CHALLENGE**

STARTING DATE:

END DATE:

**REWARD**

**I CAN MAKE IT!**

| 1 | 2 | 3 | 4 | 5 | 6 | 7 |

| 8 | 9 | 10 | 11 | 12 | 13 | 14 |

| 15 | 16 | 17 | 18 | 19 | 20 | 21 |

| 22 | 23 | 24 | 25 | 26 | 27 | 28 |

| 29 | 30 | **I DID IT!**

**NOTE**

## PLAN OF ACTION

## HOW WILL IT BENEFIT ME?

1.
2.
3.
4.
5.
6.
7.
8.
10.
11.
12.

# 30 DAYS *challenge tracker*

**CHALLENGE**

📅 STARTING DATE:

📅 END DATE:

**REWARD**

**I CAN MAKE IT!**

( 1 ) ( 2 ) ( 3 ) ( 4 ) ( 5 ) ( 6 ) ( 7 )

( 8 ) ( 9 ) ( 10 ) ( 11 ) ( 12 ) ( 13 ) ( 14 )

( 15 ) ( 16 ) ( 17 ) ( 18 ) ( 19 ) ( 20 ) ( 21 )

( 22 ) ( 23 ) ( 24 ) ( 25 ) ( 26 ) ( 27 ) ( 28 )

( 29 ) ( 30 ) **I DID IT!**

**NOTE**

**PLAN OF ACTION**

**HOW WILL IT BENEFIT ME?**

1.
2.
3.
4.
5.
6.
7.
8.
10.
11.
12.

# 30 DAYS *challenge tracker*

**CHALLENGE**

📅 STARTING DATE:

📅 END DATE:

**REWARD**

I CAN MAKE IT!

( 1 ) ( 2 ) ( 3 ) ( 4 ) ( 5 ) ( 6 ) ( 7 )

( 8 ) ( 9 ) ( 10 ) ( 11 ) ( 12 ) ( 13 ) ( 14 )

( 15 ) ( 16 ) ( 17 ) ( 18 ) ( 19 ) ( 20 ) ( 21 )

( 22 ) ( 23 ) ( 24 ) ( 25 ) ( 26 ) ( 27 ) ( 28 )

( 29 ) ( 30 ) I DID IT!

**NOTE**

**PLAN OF ACTION**

**HOW WILL IT BENEFIT ME?**

1.
2.
3.
4.
5.
6.
7.
8.
10.
11.
12.

# 30 DAYS *challenge tracker*

**CHALLENGE**

STARTING DATE:

END DATE:

**REWARD**

**I CAN MAKE IT!**

1 — 2 — 3 — 4 — 5 — 6 — 7

8 — 9 — 10 — 11 — 12 — 13 — 14

15 — 16 — 17 — 18 — 19 — 20 — 21

22 — 23 — 24 — 25 — 26 — 27 — 28

29 — 30 — **I DID IT!**

**NOTE**

**PLAN OF ACTION**

**HOW WILL IT BENEFIT ME?**

1.
2.
3.
4.
5.
6.
7.
8.
10.
11.
12.

# 30 DAYS *challenge tracker*

**CHALLENGE**

📅 STARTING DATE:

📅 END DATE:

**REWARD**

I CAN MAKE IT!

(1) (2) (3) (4) (5) (6) (7)

(8) (9) (10) (11) (12) (13) (14)

(15) (16) (17) (18) (19) (20) (21)

(22) (23) (24) (25) (26) (27) (28)

(29) (30) I DID IT!

**NOTE**

**PLAN OF ACTION**

**HOW WILL IT BENEFIT ME?**

1.
2.
3.
4.
5.
6.
7.
8.
10.
11.
12.

# 30 DAYS *challenge tracker*

**CHALLENGE**

STARTING DATE:

END DATE:

**REWARD**

**I CAN MAKE IT!**

( 1 ) ( 2 ) ( 3 ) ( 4 ) ( 5 ) ( 6 ) ( 7 )

( 8 ) ( 9 ) ( 10 ) ( 11 ) ( 12 ) ( 13 ) ( 14 )

( 15 ) ( 16 ) ( 17 ) ( 18 ) ( 19 ) ( 20 ) ( 21 )

( 22 ) ( 23 ) ( 24 ) ( 25 ) ( 26 ) ( 27 ) ( 28 )

( 29 ) ( 30 ) **I DID IT!**

**NOTE**

**PLAN OF ACTION**

**HOW WILL IT BENEFIT ME?**

1.
2.
3.
4.
5.
6.
7.
8.
10.
11.
12.

# 30 DAYS *challenge tracker*

**CHALLENGE**

📅 STARTING DATE:

📅 END DATE:

**REWARD**

**I CAN MAKE IT!**

( 1 ) ( 2 ) ( 3 ) ( 4 ) ( 5 ) ( 6 ) ( 7 )

( 8 ) ( 9 ) ( 10 ) ( 11 ) ( 12 ) ( 13 ) ( 14 )

( 15 ) ( 16 ) ( 17 ) ( 18 ) ( 19 ) ( 20 ) ( 21 )

( 22 ) ( 23 ) ( 24 ) ( 25 ) ( 26 ) ( 27 ) ( 28 )

( 29 ) ( 30 ) **I DID IT!**

**NOTE**

**PLAN OF ACTION**

**HOW WILL IT BENEFIT ME?**

1.
2.
3.
4.
5.
6.
7.
8.
10.
11.
12.

# 30 DAYS *challenge tracker*

**CHALLENGE**

**STARTING DATE:**

**END DATE:**

**REWARD**

I CAN MAKE IT!

( 1 ) ( 2 ) ( 3 ) ( 4 ) ( 5 ) ( 6 ) ( 7 )

( 8 ) ( 9 ) ( 10 ) ( 11 ) ( 12 ) ( 13 ) ( 14 )

( 15 ) ( 16 ) ( 17 ) ( 18 ) ( 19 ) ( 20 ) ( 21 )

( 22 ) ( 23 ) ( 24 ) ( 25 ) ( 26 ) ( 27 ) ( 28 )

( 29 ) ( 30 ) I DID IT!

**NOTE**

**PLAN OF ACTION**

**HOW WILL IT BENEFIT ME?**

1.
2.
3.
4.
5.
6.
7.
8.
10.
11.
12.

# 30 DAYS *challenge tracker*

**CHALLENGE**

📅 STARTING DATE:

📅 END DATE:

**REWARD**

I CAN MAKE IT!

| 1 | 2 | 3 | 4 | 5 | 6 | 7 |

| 8 | 9 | 10 | 11 | 12 | 13 | 14 |

| 15 | 16 | 17 | 18 | 19 | 20 | 21 |

| 22 | 23 | 24 | 25 | 26 | 27 | 28 |

29 | 30 | I DID IT!

**NOTE**

**PLAN OF ACTION**

**HOW WILL IT BENEFIT ME?**

1.
2.
3.
4.
5.
6.
7.
8.
10.
11.
12.

# 30 DAYS *challenge tracker*

**CHALLENGE**

STARTING DATE:

END DATE:

**REWARD**

I CAN MAKE IT!

| 1 | 2 | 3 | 4 | 5 | 6 | 7 |

| 8 | 9 | 10 | 11 | 12 | 13 | 14 |

| 15 | 16 | 17 | 18 | 19 | 20 | 21 |

| 22 | 23 | 24 | 25 | 26 | 27 | 28 |

| 29 | 30 | I DID IT! |

**NOTE**

**PLAN OF ACTION**

**HOW WILL IT BENEFIT ME?**

1.
2.
3.
4.
5.
6.
7.
8.
10.
11.
12.

# 30 DAYS *challenge tracker*

CHALLENGE

REWARD

📅 STARTING DATE:

📅 END DATE:

I CAN MAKE IT!

( 1 )—( 2 )—( 3 )—( 4 )—( 5 )—( 6 )—( 7 )

( 8 )—( 9 )—( 10 )—( 11 )—( 12 )—( 13 )—( 14 )

( 15 )—( 16 )—( 17 )—( 18 )—( 19 )—( 20 )—( 21 )

( 22 )—( 23 )—( 24 )—( 25 )—( 26 )—( 27 )—( 28 )

( 29 )—( 30 ) I DID IT!

NOTE

PLAN OF ACTION

HOW WILL IT BENEFIT ME?

1.
2.
3.
4.
5.
6.
7.
8.
10.
11.
12.

# 30 DAYS *challenge tracker*

**CHALLENGE**

📅 STARTING DATE:

📅 END DATE:

**REWARD**

I CAN MAKE IT!

( 1 ) ( 2 ) ( 3 ) ( 4 ) ( 5 ) ( 6 ) ( 7 )

( 8 ) ( 9 ) ( 10 ) ( 11 ) ( 12 ) ( 13 ) ( 14 )

( 15 ) ( 16 ) ( 17 ) ( 18 ) ( 19 ) ( 20 ) ( 21 )

( 22 ) ( 23 ) ( 24 ) ( 25 ) ( 26 ) ( 27 ) ( 28 )

( 29 ) ( 30 ) I DID IT!

**NOTE**

**PLAN OF ACTION**

**HOW WILL IT BENEFIT ME?**

1.
2.
3.
4.
5.
6.
7.
8.
10.
11.
12.

# 30 DAYS *challenge tracker*

**CHALLENGE**

📅 STARTING DATE:

📅 END DATE:

**REWARD**

**I CAN MAKE IT!**

( 1 )—( 2 )—( 3 )—( 4 )—( 5 )—( 6 )—( 7 )

( 8 )—( 9 )—( 10 )—( 11 )—( 12 )—( 13 )—( 14 )

( 15 )—( 16 )—( 17 )—( 18 )—( 19 )—( 20 )—( 21 )

( 22 )—( 23 )—( 24 )—( 25 )—( 26 )—( 27 )—( 28 )

( 29 )—( 30 ) **I DID IT!**

**NOTE**

## PLAN OF ACTION

- 
- 
- 
- 
- 
- 
- 
- 

## HOW WILL IT BENEFIT ME?

1.
2.
3.
4.
5.
6.
7.
8.
10.
11.
12.

# 30 DAYS *challenge tracker*

**CHALLENGE**

📅 STARTING DATE:

📅 END DATE:

**REWARD**

**I CAN MAKE IT!**

( 1 ) ( 2 ) ( 3 ) ( 4 ) ( 5 ) ( 6 ) ( 7 )

( 8 ) ( 9 ) ( 10 ) ( 11 ) ( 12 ) ( 13 ) ( 14 )

( 15 ) ( 16 ) ( 17 ) ( 18 ) ( 19 ) ( 20 ) ( 21 )

( 22 ) ( 23 ) ( 24 ) ( 25 ) ( 26 ) ( 27 ) ( 28 )

( 29 ) ( 30 ) **I DID IT!**

**NOTE**

**PLAN OF ACTION**

**HOW WILL IT BENEFIT ME?**

1.
2.
3.
4.
5.
6.
7.
8.
10.
11.
12.

# 30 DAYS *challenge tracker*

**CHALLENGE**

STARTING DATE:

END DATE:

**REWARD**

I CAN MAKE IT!

| 1 | 2 | 3 | 4 | 5 | 6 | 7 |
|---|---|---|---|---|---|---|
| 8 | 9 | 10 | 11 | 12 | 13 | 14 |
| 15 | 16 | 17 | 18 | 19 | 20 | 21 |
| 22 | 23 | 24 | 25 | 26 | 27 | 28 |

29  30  I DID IT!

**NOTE**

**PLAN OF ACTION**

**HOW WILL IT BENEFIT ME?**

1.
2.
3.
4.
5.
6.
7.
8.
10.
11.
12.

# 30 DAYS *challenge tracker*

**CHALLENGE**

📅 STARTING DATE:

📅 END DATE:

**REWARD**

**I CAN MAKE IT!**

( 1 )  ( 2 )  ( 3 )  ( 4 )  ( 5 )  ( 6 )  ( 7 )

( 8 )  ( 9 )  ( 10 )  ( 11 )  ( 12 )  ( 13 )  ( 14 )

( 15 )  ( 16 )  ( 17 )  ( 18 )  ( 19 )  ( 20 )  ( 21 )

( 22 )  ( 23 )  ( 24 )  ( 25 )  ( 26 )  ( 27 )  ( 28 )

( 29 )  ( 30 )  **I DID IT!**

**NOTE**

**PLAN OF ACTION**

**HOW WILL IT BENEFIT ME?**

1.
2.
3.
4.
5.
6.
7.
8.
10.
11.
12.

# 30 DAYS *challenge tracker*

CHALLENGE

STARTING DATE:

END DATE:

REWARD

I CAN MAKE IT!

| 1 | 2 | 3 | 4 | 5 | 6 | 7 |
| 8 | 9 | 10 | 11 | 12 | 13 | 14 |
| 15 | 16 | 17 | 18 | 19 | 20 | 21 |
| 22 | 23 | 24 | 25 | 26 | 27 | 28 |
| 29 | 30 |

I DID IT!

NOTE

PLAN OF ACTION

HOW WILL IT BENEFIT ME?

1.
2.
3.
4.
5.
6.
7.
8.
10.
11.
12.

# 30 DAYS *challenge tracker*

**CHALLENGE**

📅 STARTING DATE:

📅 END DATE:

**REWARD**

**I CAN MAKE IT!**

( 1 ) — ( 2 ) — ( 3 ) — ( 4 ) — ( 5 ) — ( 6 ) — ( 7 )

( 8 ) — ( 9 ) — ( 10 ) — ( 11 ) — ( 12 ) — ( 13 ) — ( 14 )

( 15 ) — ( 16 ) — ( 17 ) — ( 18 ) — ( 19 ) — ( 20 ) — ( 21 )

( 22 ) — ( 23 ) — ( 24 ) — ( 25 ) — ( 26 ) — ( 27 ) — ( 28 )

( 29 ) — ( 30 )   **I DID IT!**

**NOTE**

**PLAN OF ACTION**

**HOW WILL IT BENEFIT ME?**

1.
2.
3.
4.
5.
6.
7.
8.
10.
11.
12.

# 30 DAYS *challenge tracker*

**CHALLENGE**

📅 STARTING DATE:

📅 END DATE:

**REWARD**

I CAN MAKE IT!

( 1 )—( 2 )—( 3 )—( 4 )—( 5 )—( 6 )—( 7 )

( 8 )—( 9 )—( 10 )—( 11 )—( 12 )—( 13 )—( 14 )

( 15 )—( 16 )—( 17 )—( 18 )—( 19 )—( 20 )—( 21 )

( 22 )—( 23 )—( 24 )—( 25 )—( 26 )—( 27 )—( 28 )

( 29 )—( 30 ) I DID IT!

**NOTE**

**PLAN OF ACTION**

**HOW WILL IT BENEFIT ME?**

1.
2.
3.
4.
5.
6.
7.
8.
10.
11.
12.